THE COLORING BOOK BELONGS TO

_____ _____

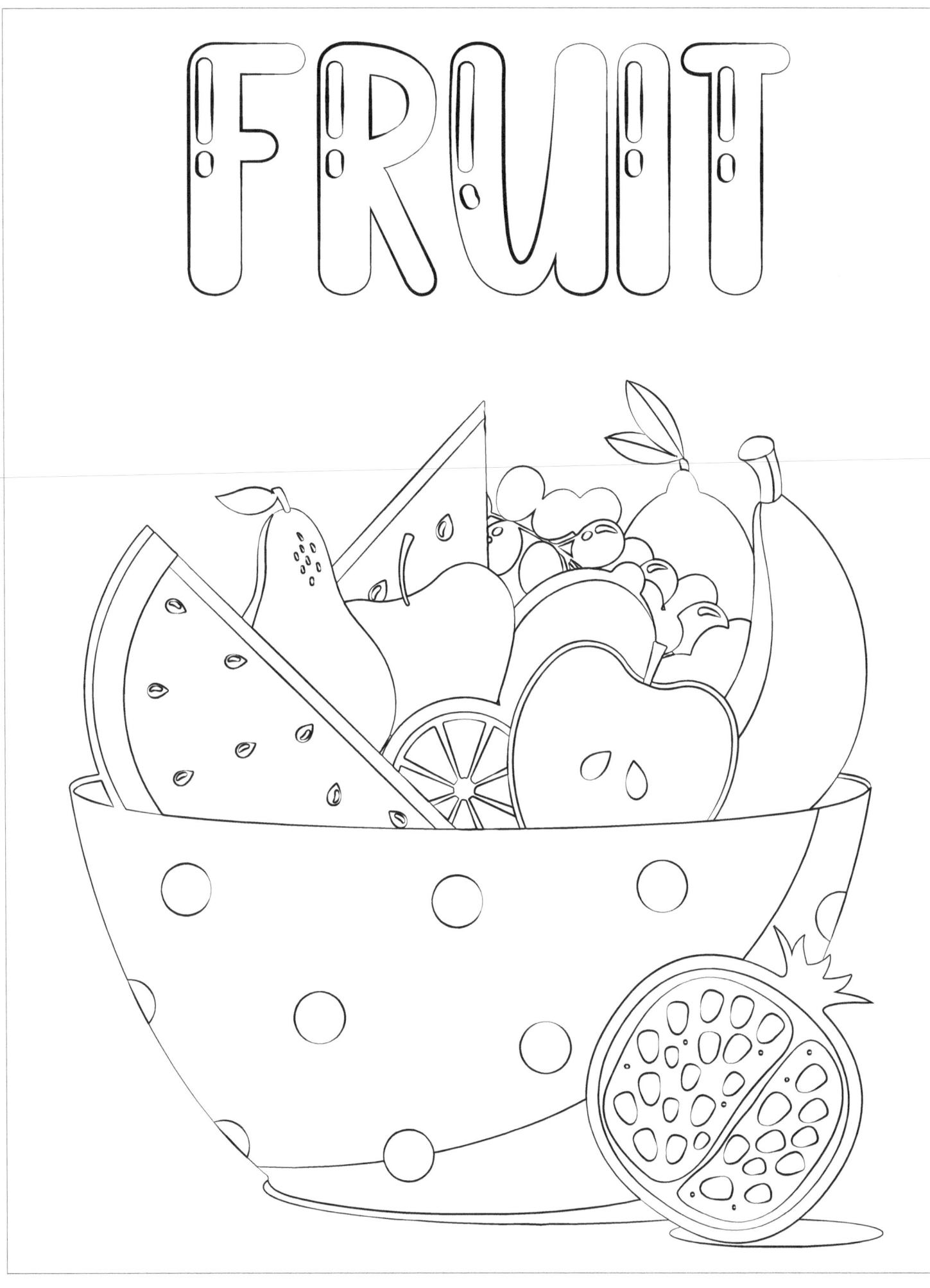

BANANA

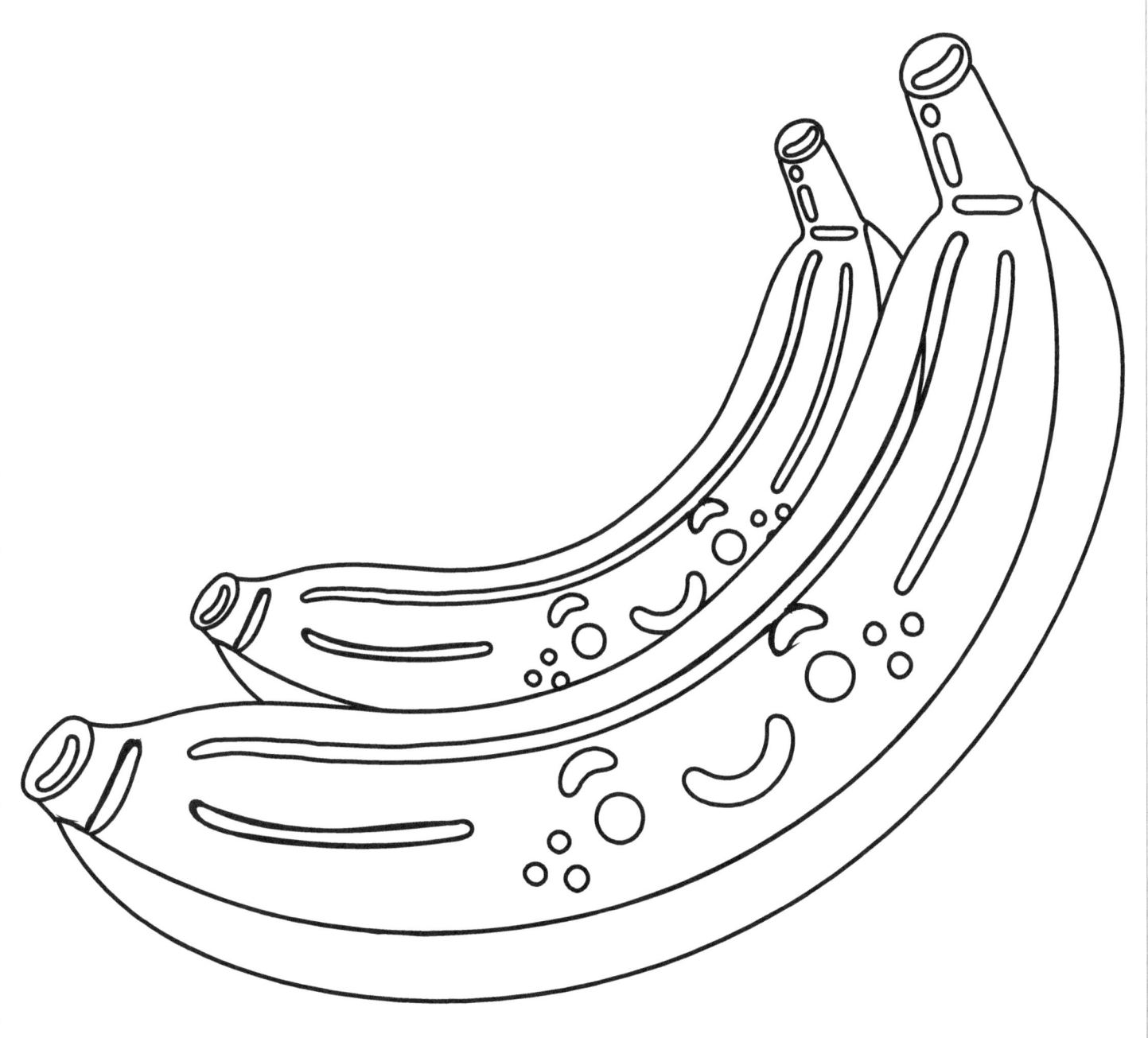

PEAR

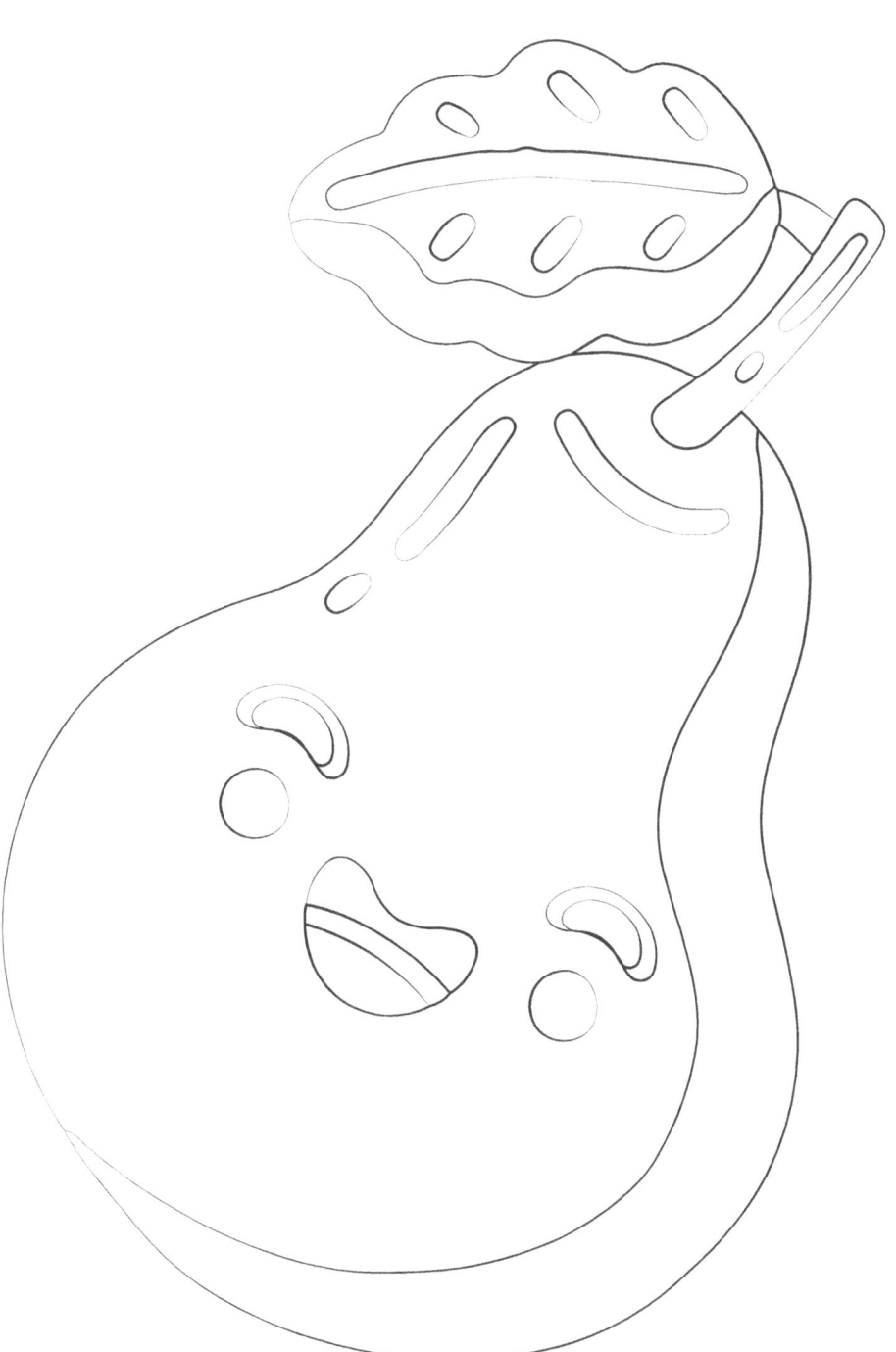

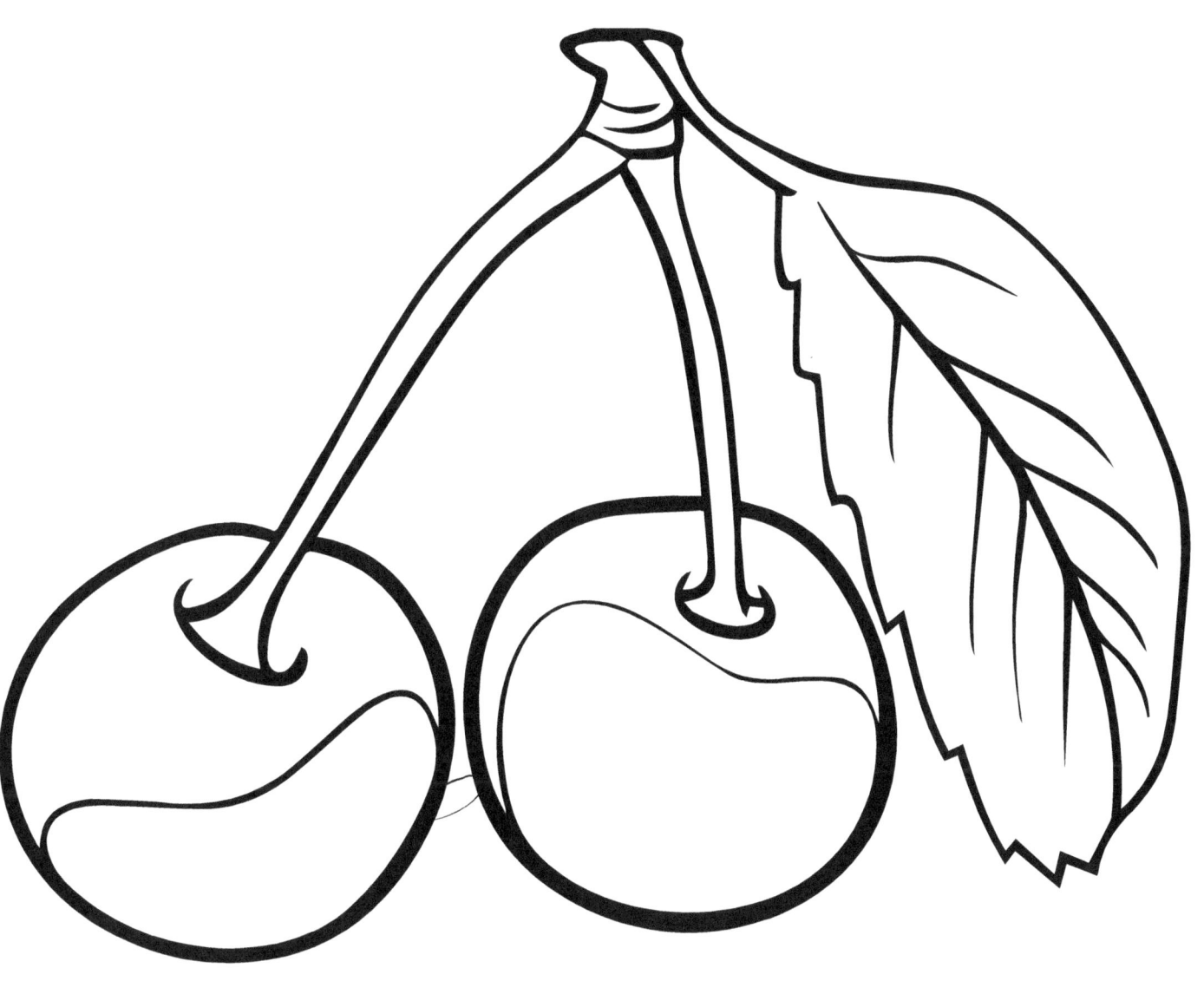

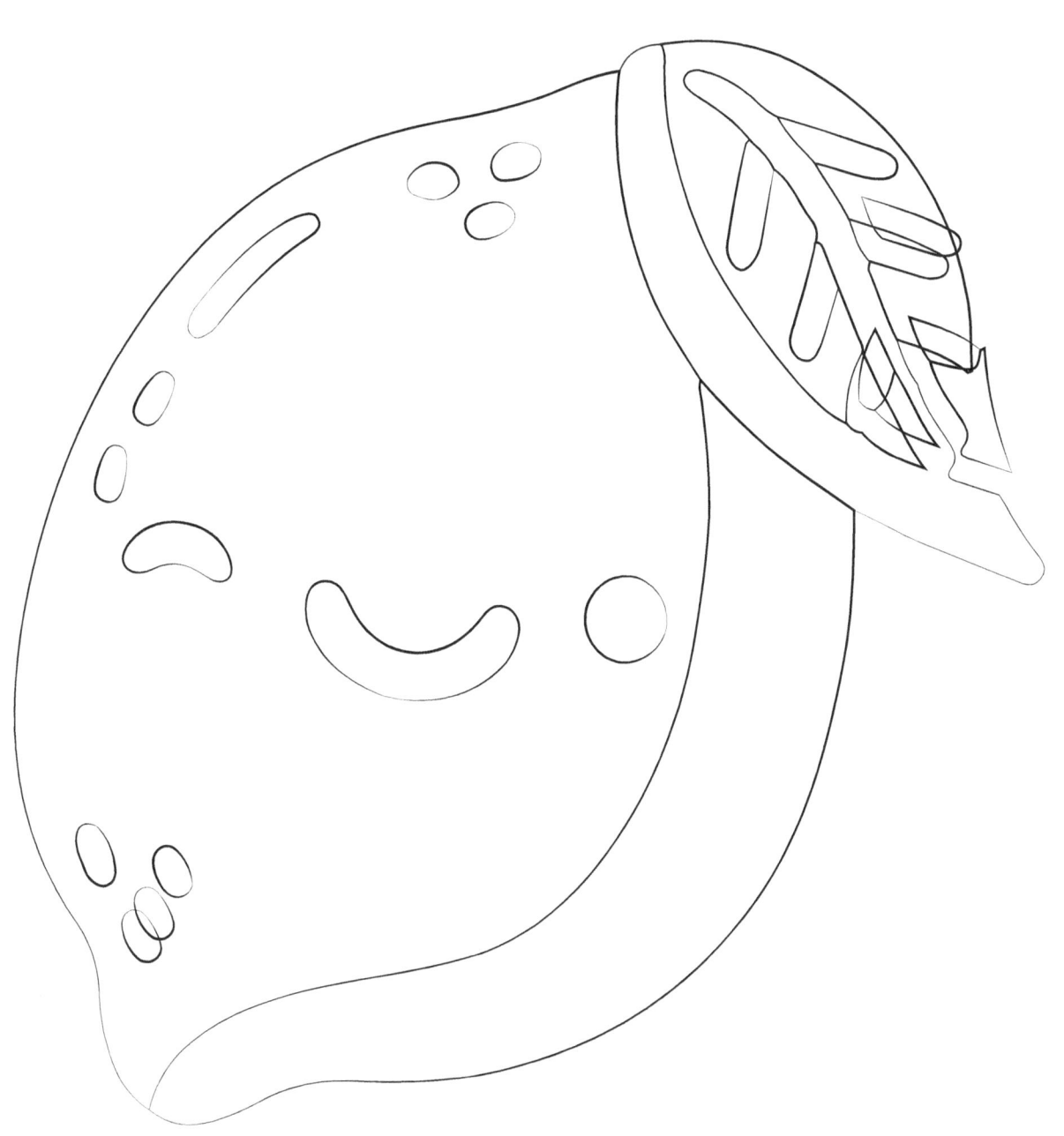

STRAWBERRY

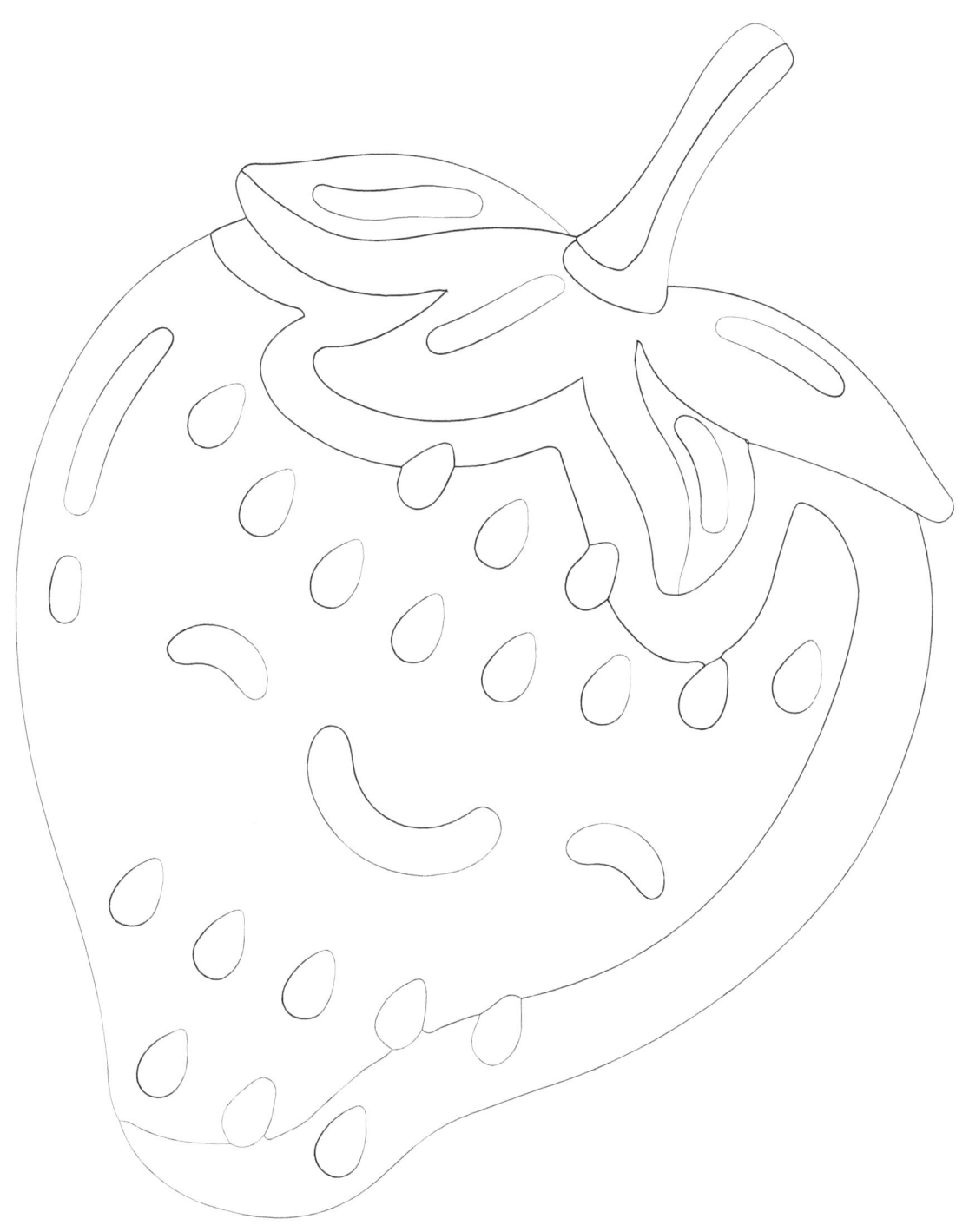

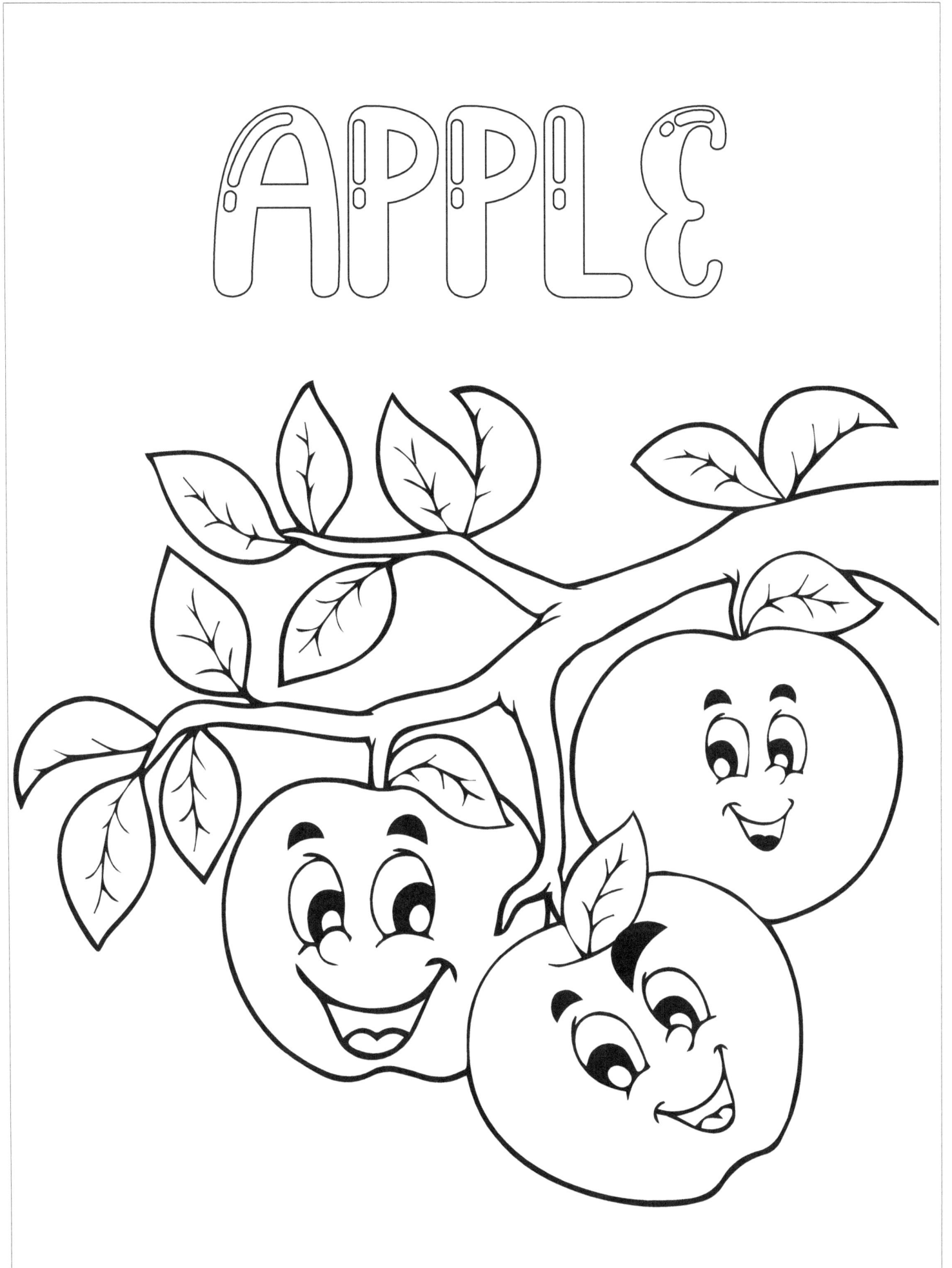

GRAPE

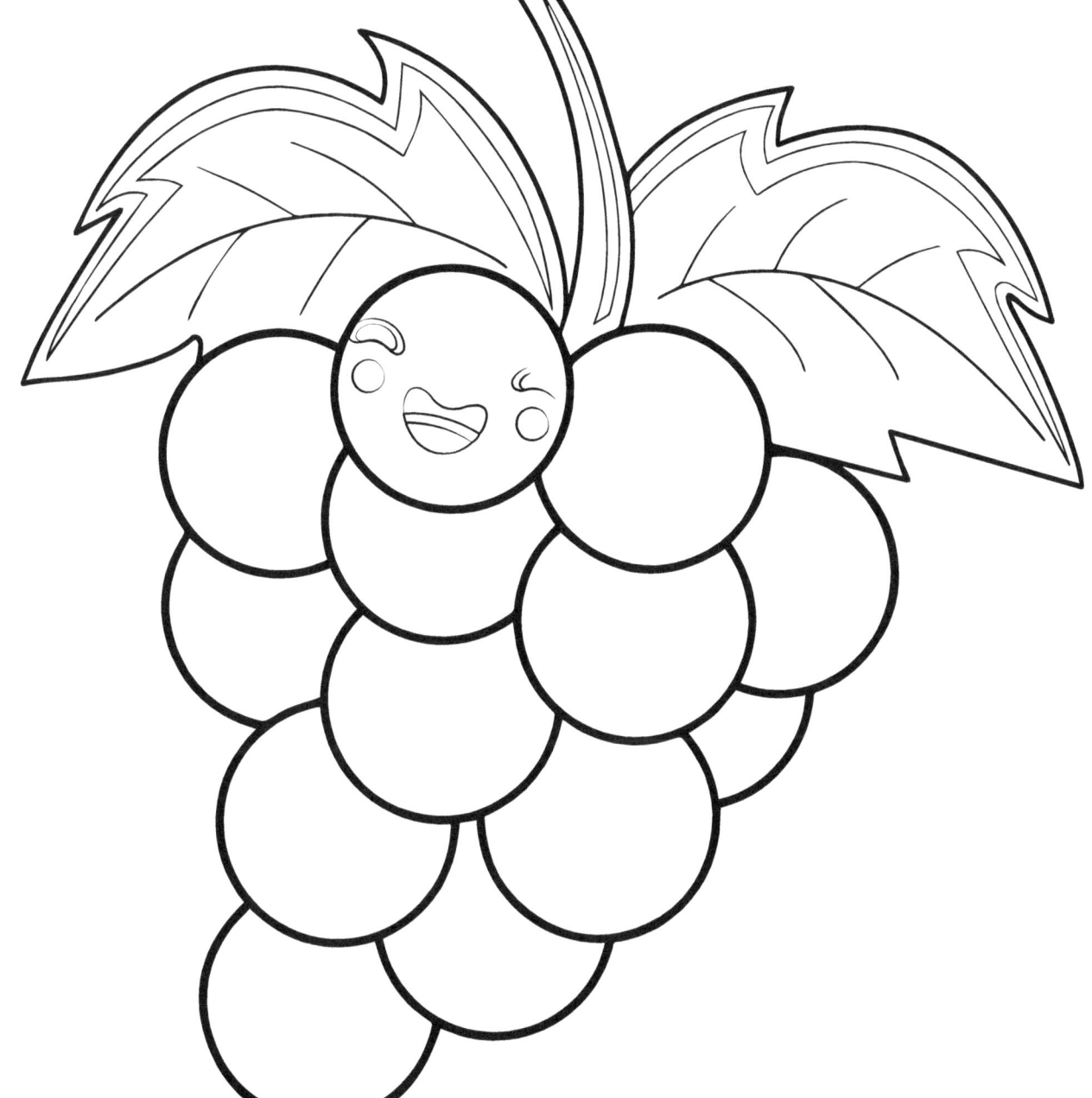

MANGOSTEEN

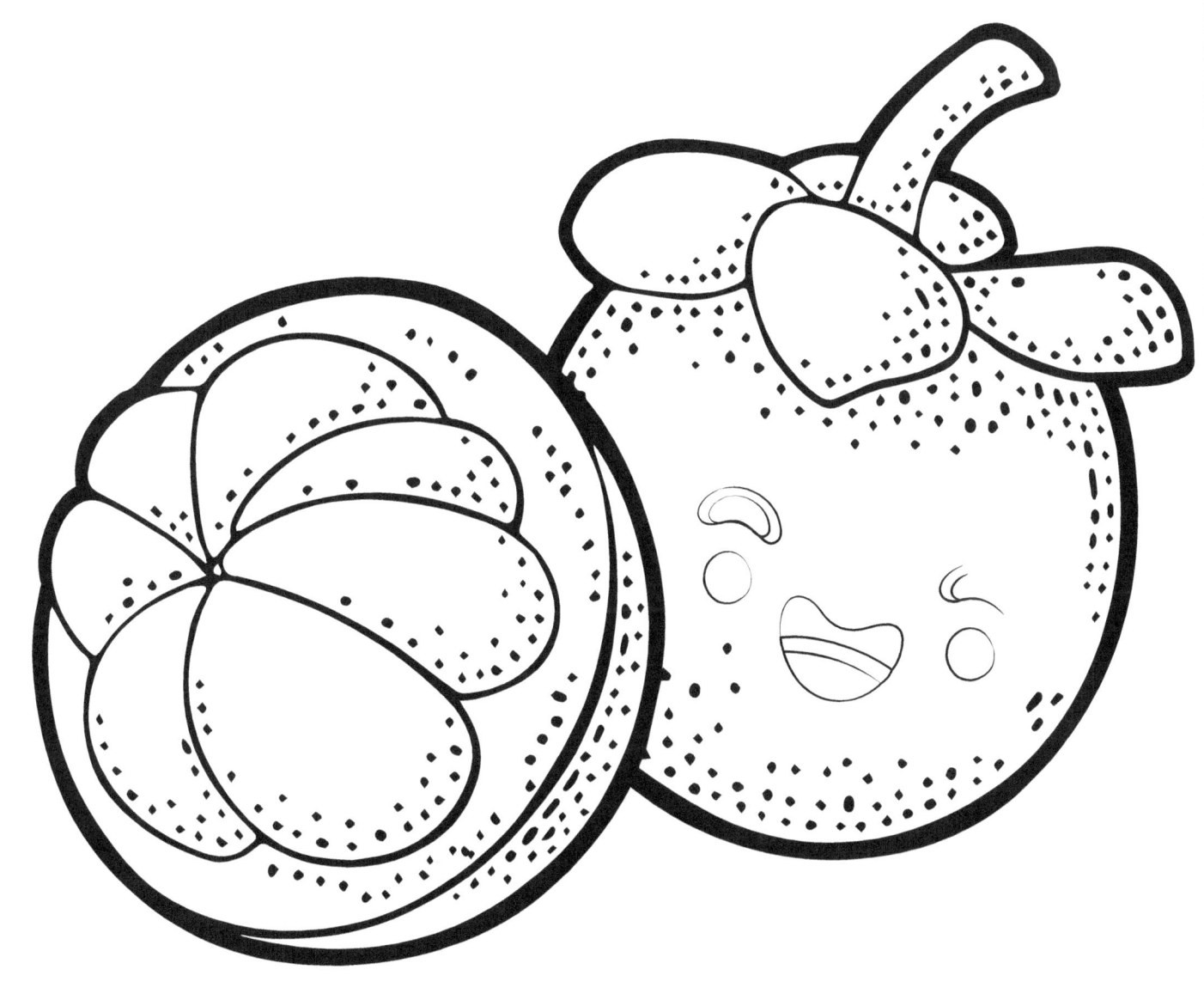

PITAYA

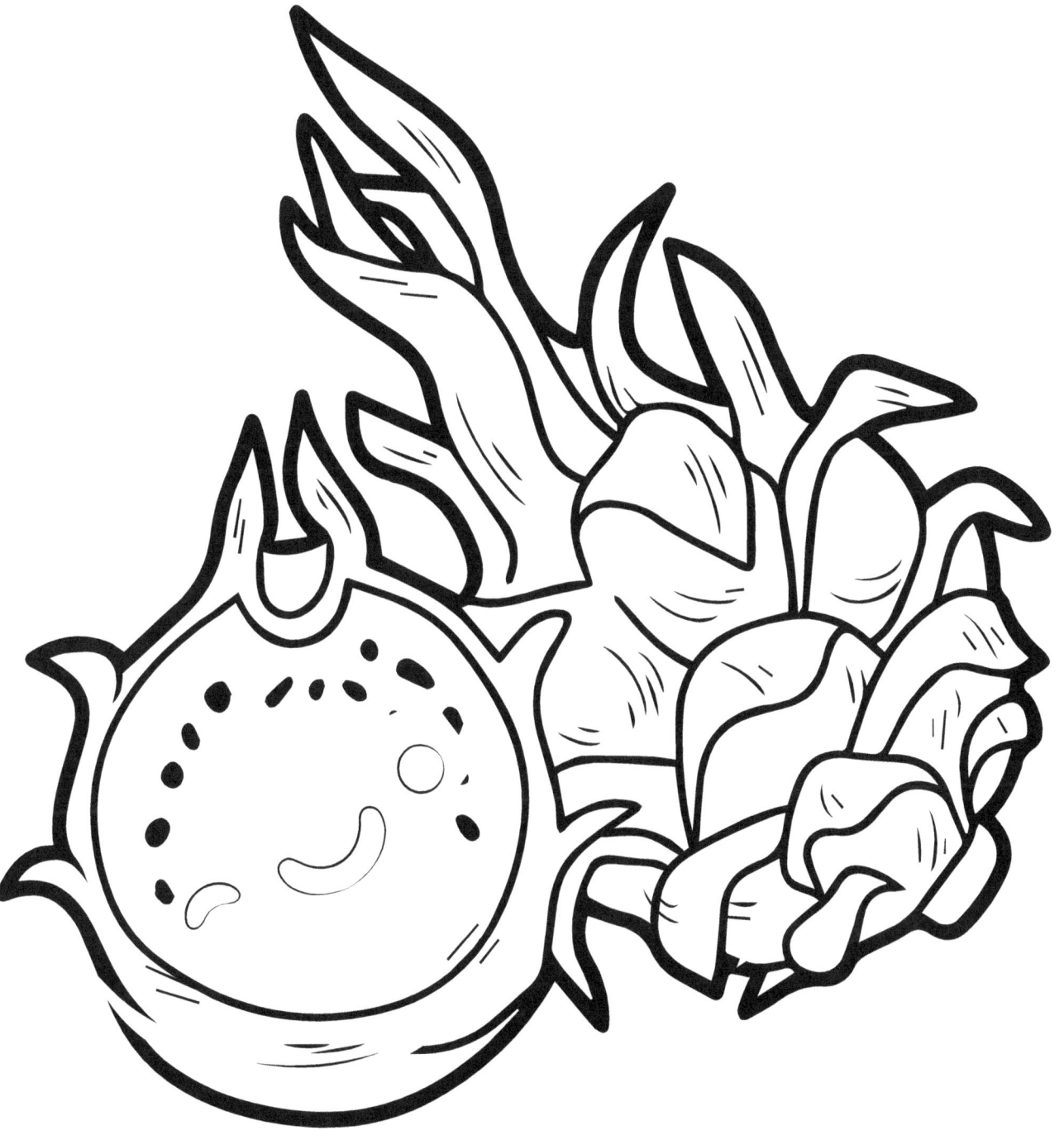

WATERMELON

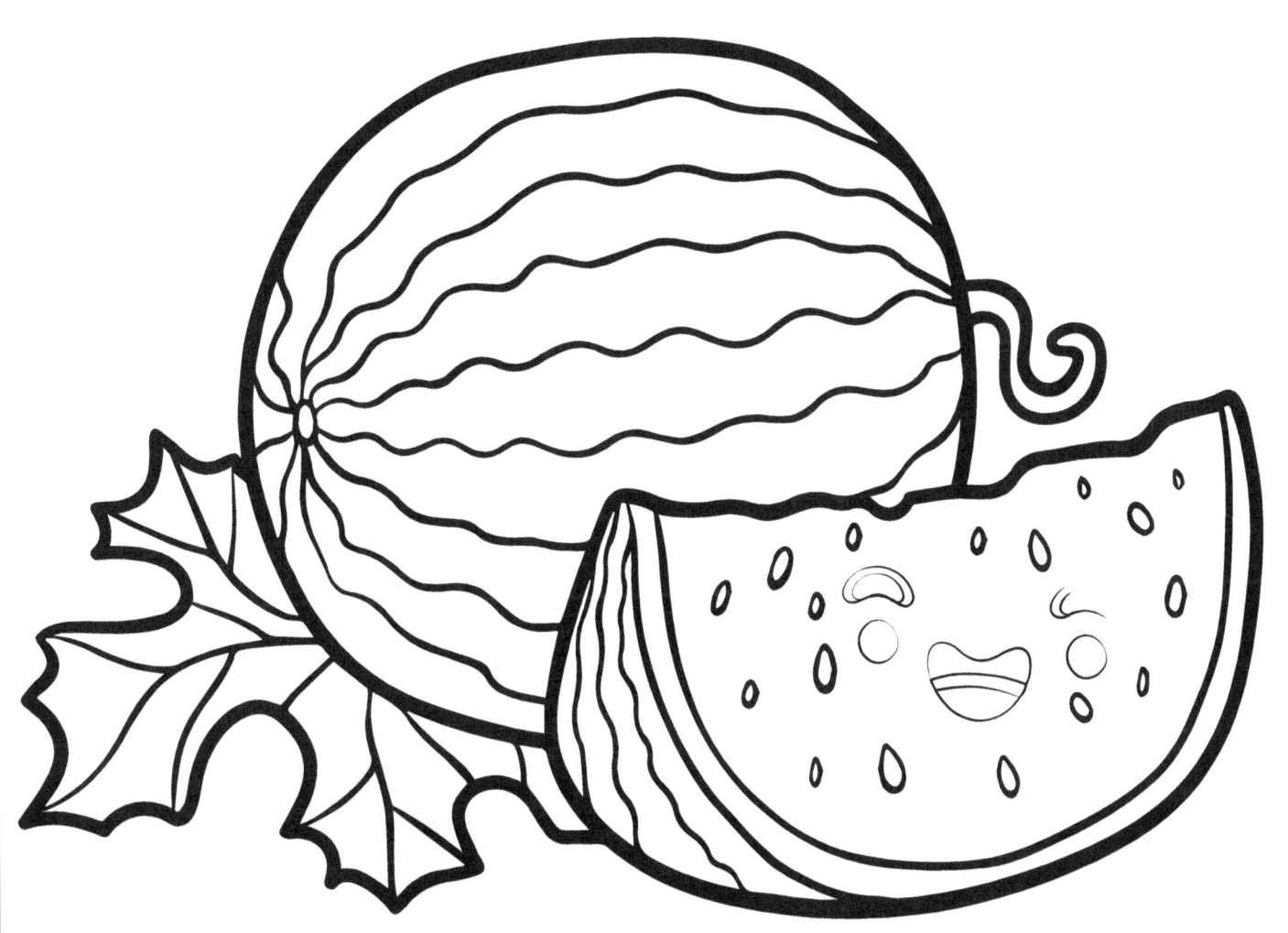

PINEAPPLE

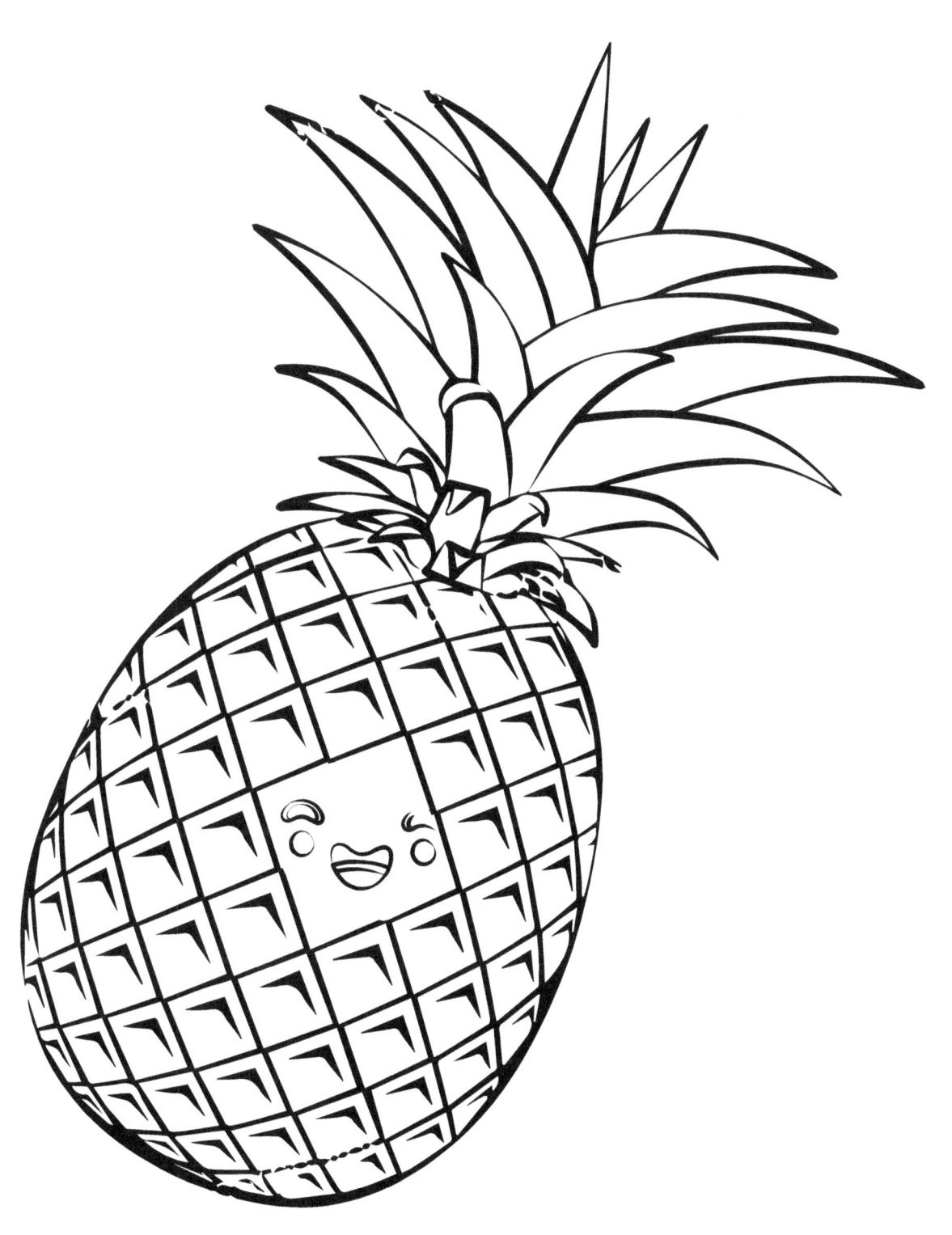

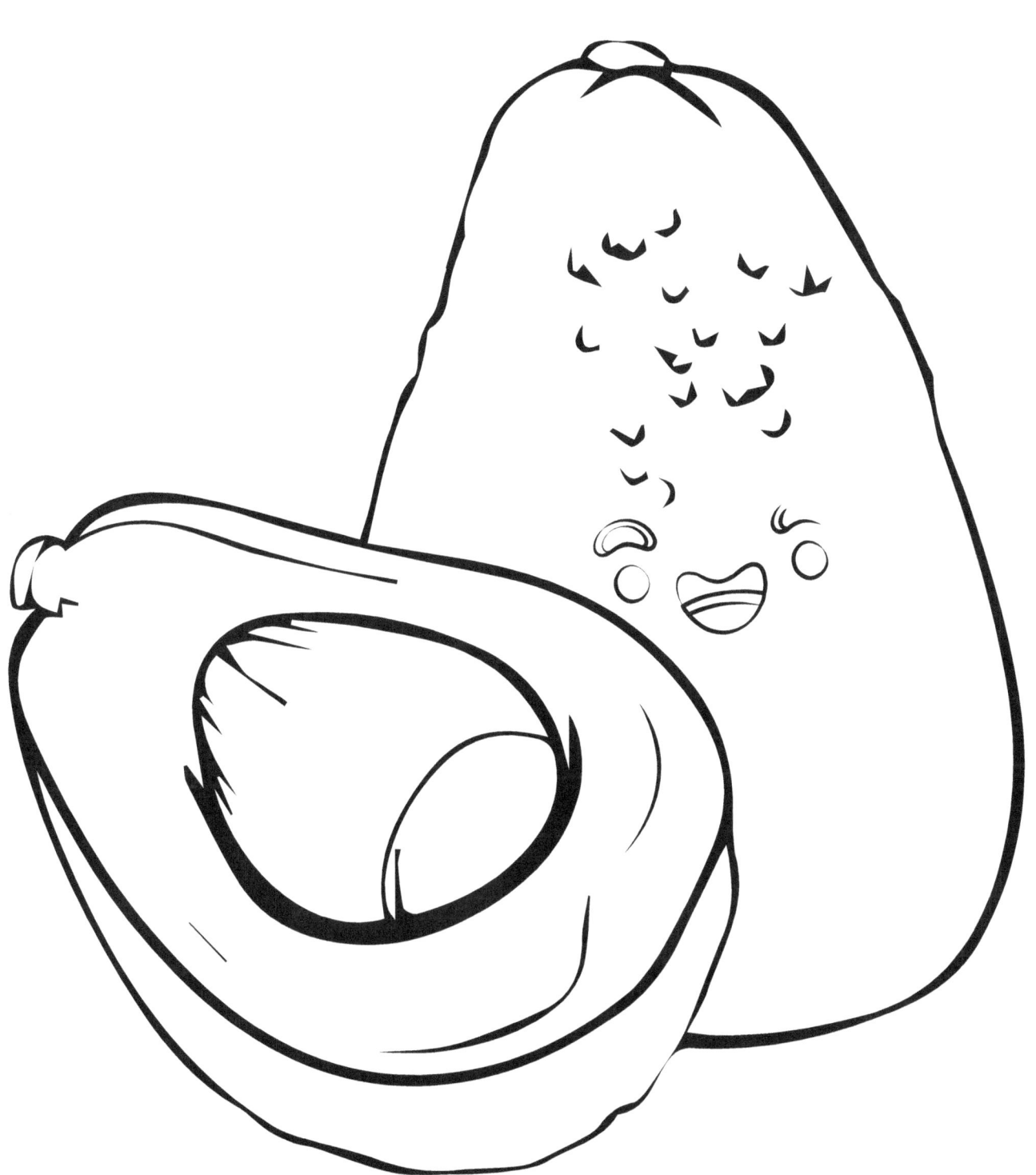

BLUEBERRY

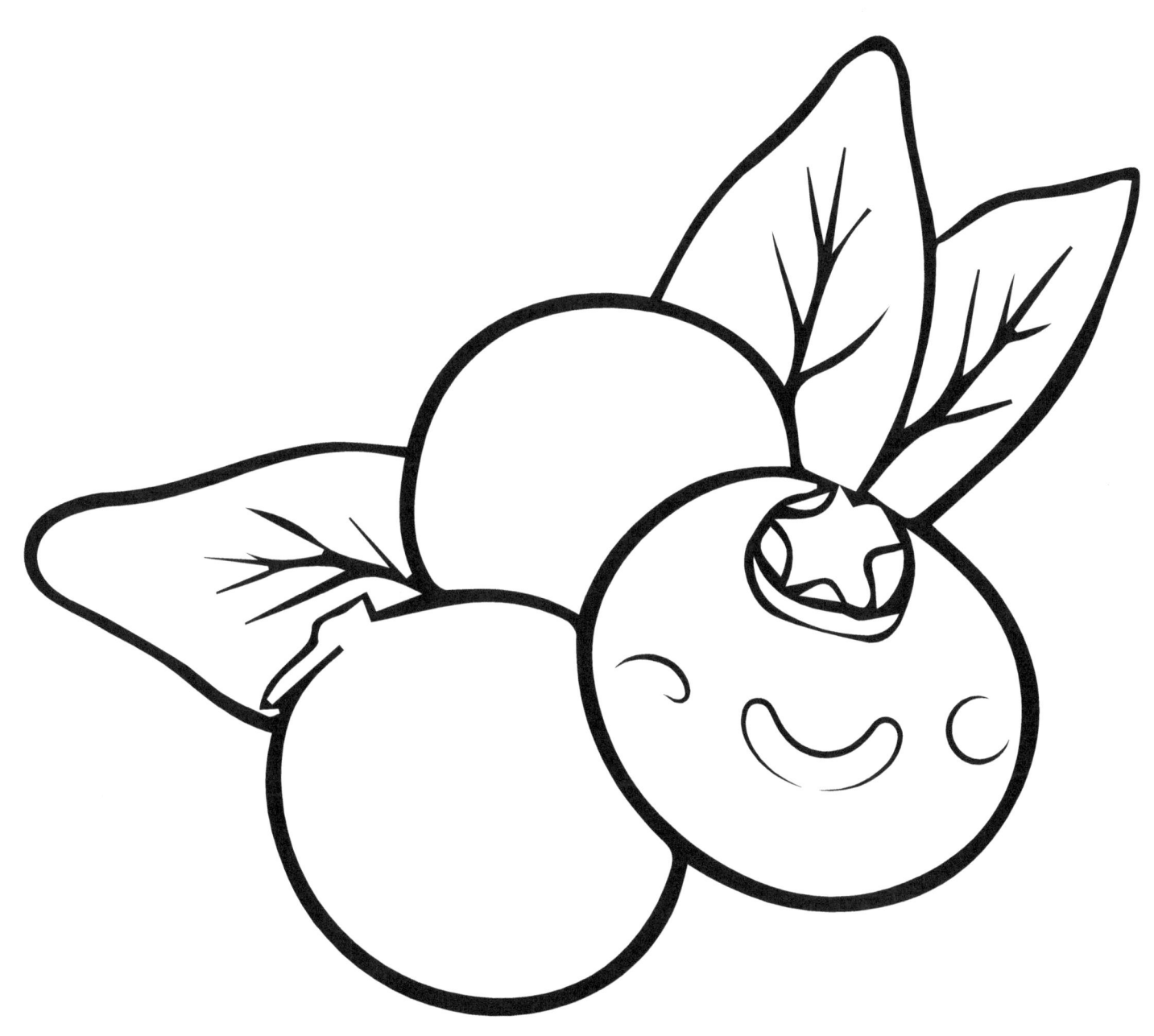

APRICOT

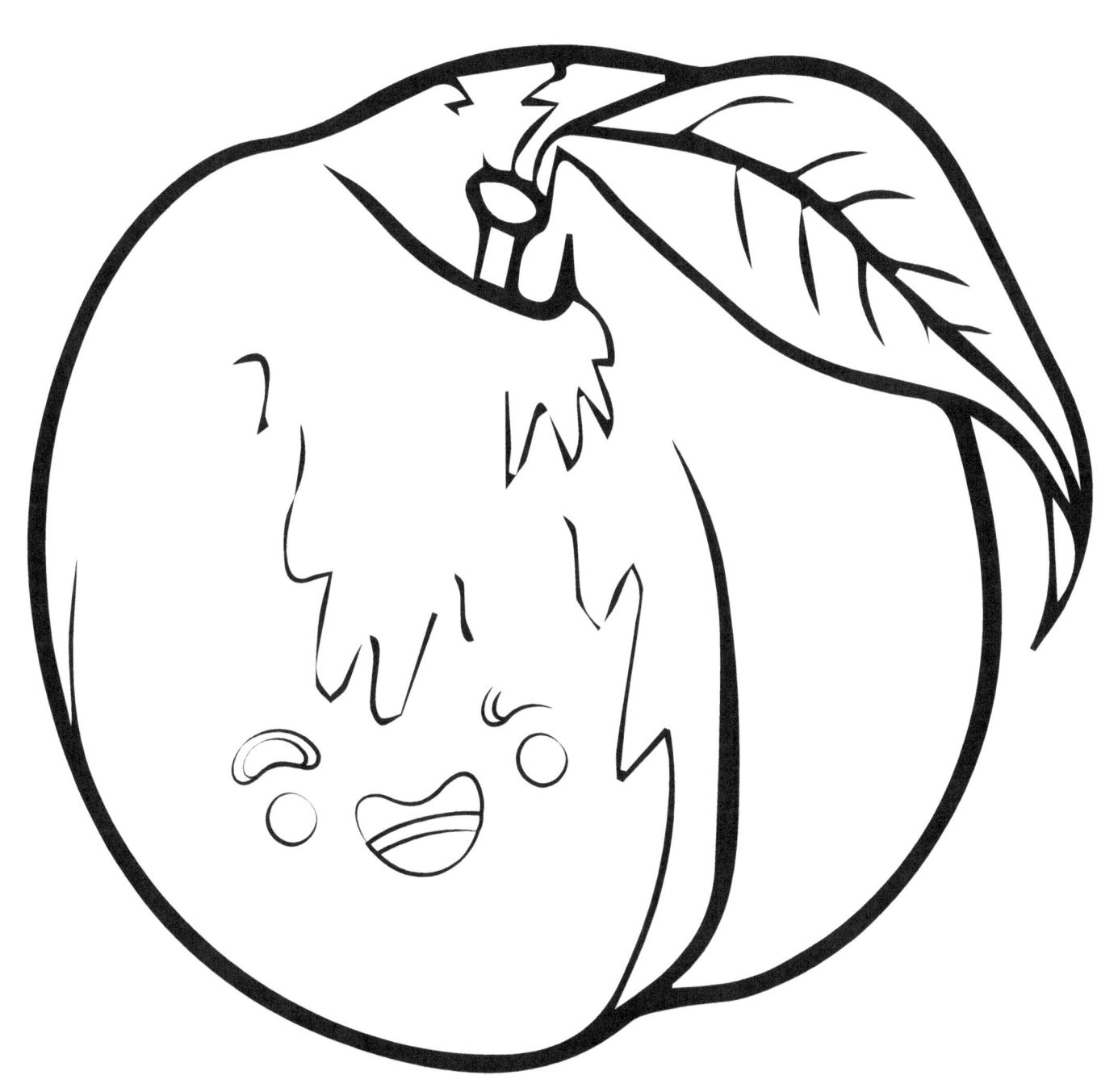

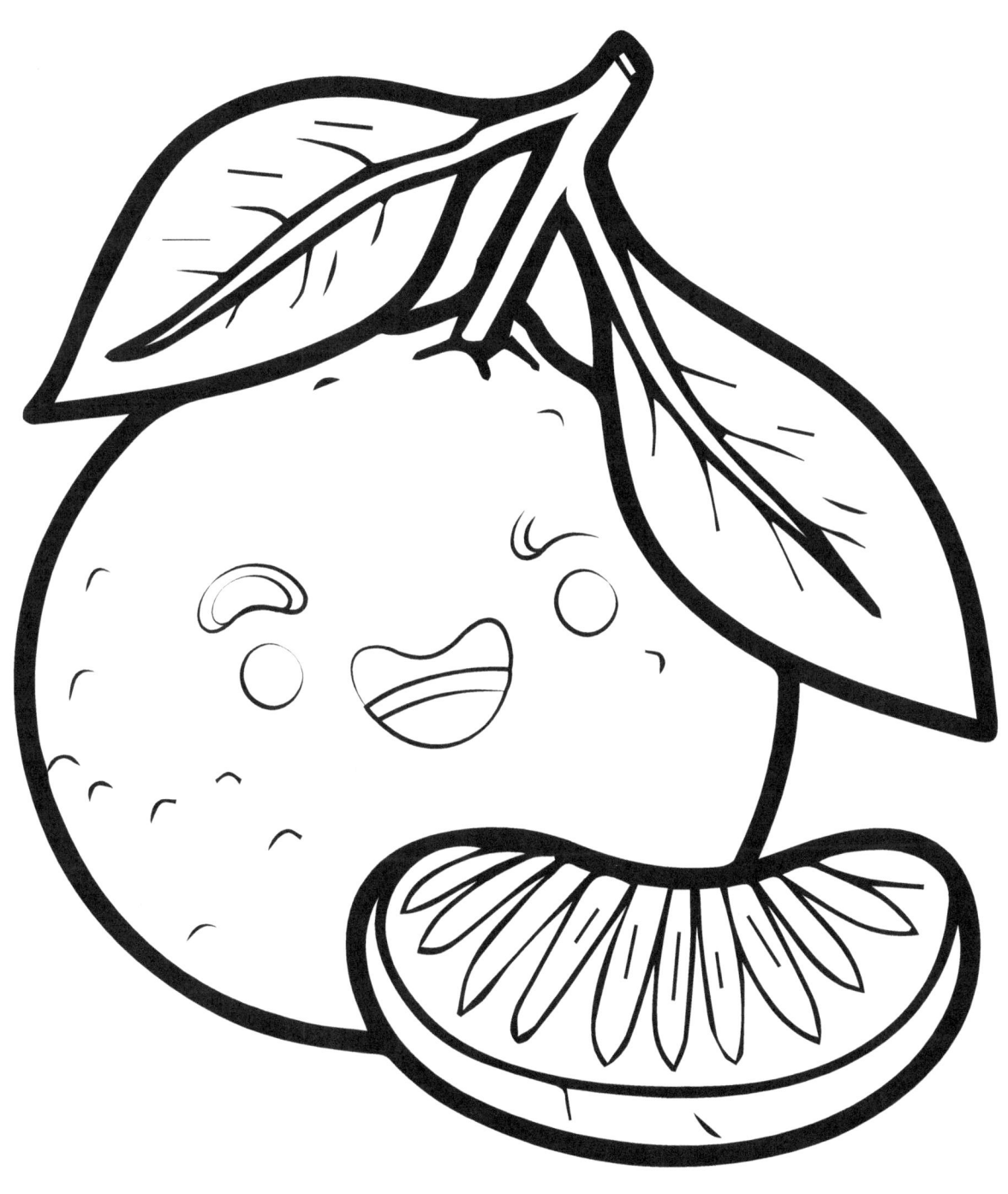

MANGO

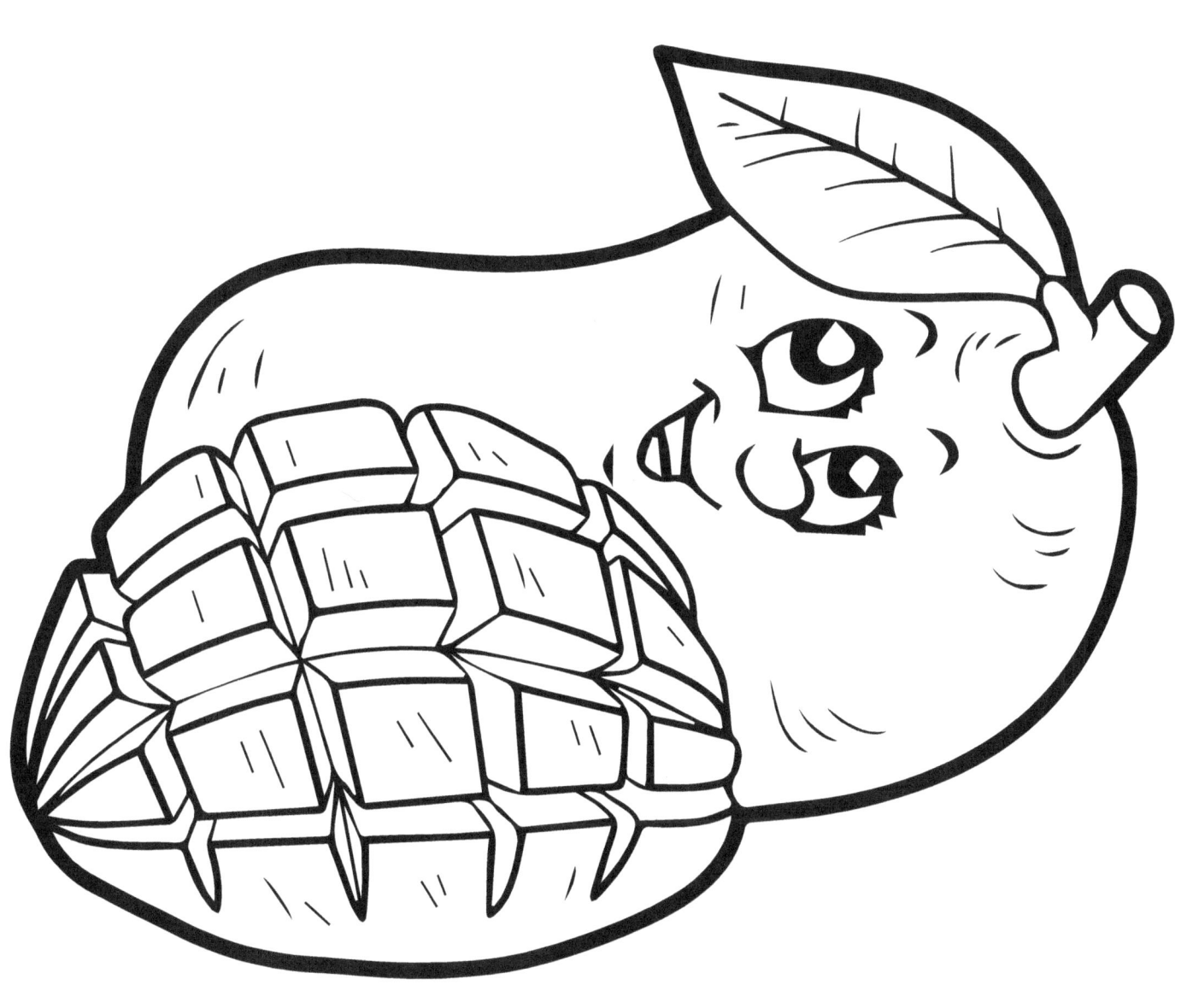

KIWI

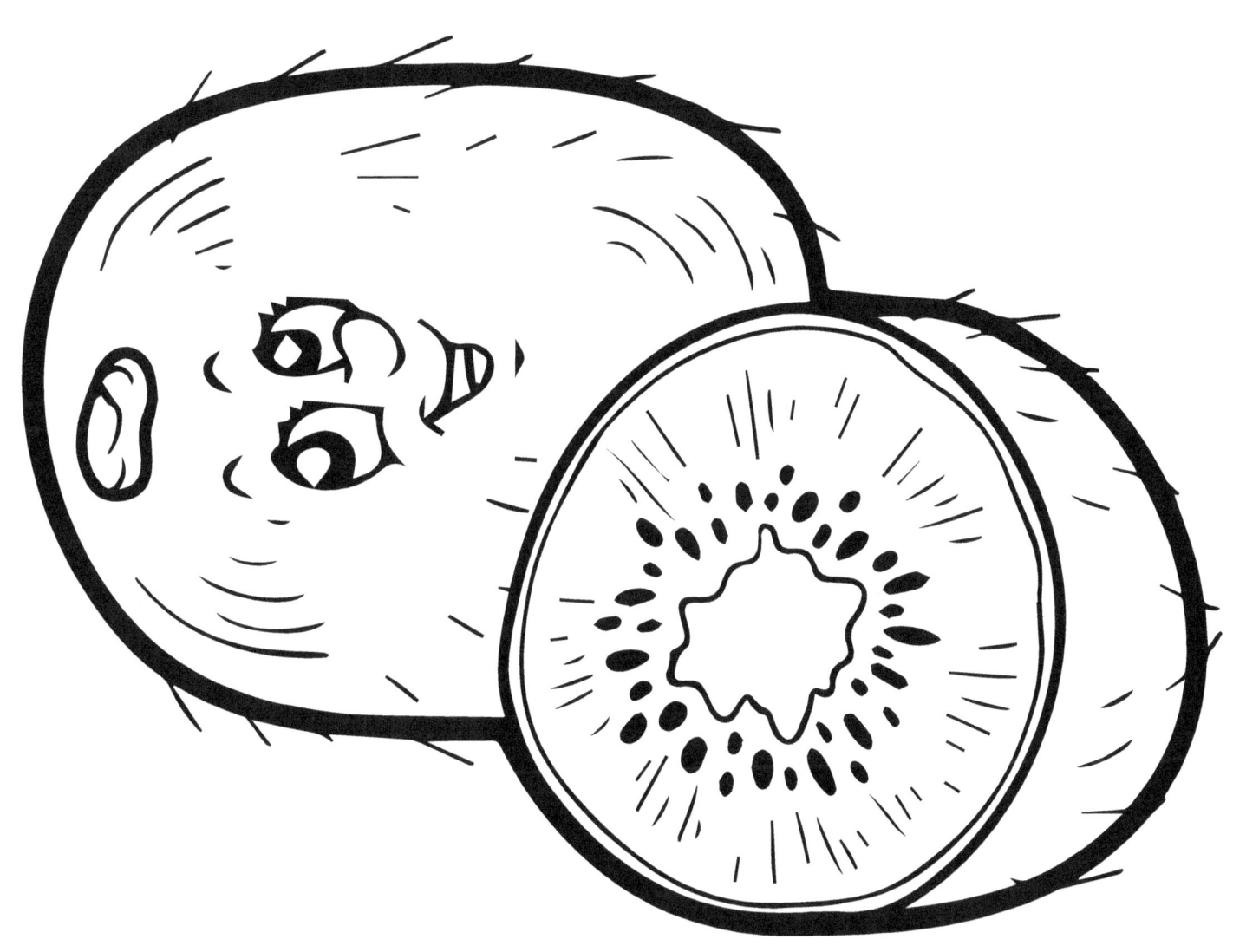

PAPAYA

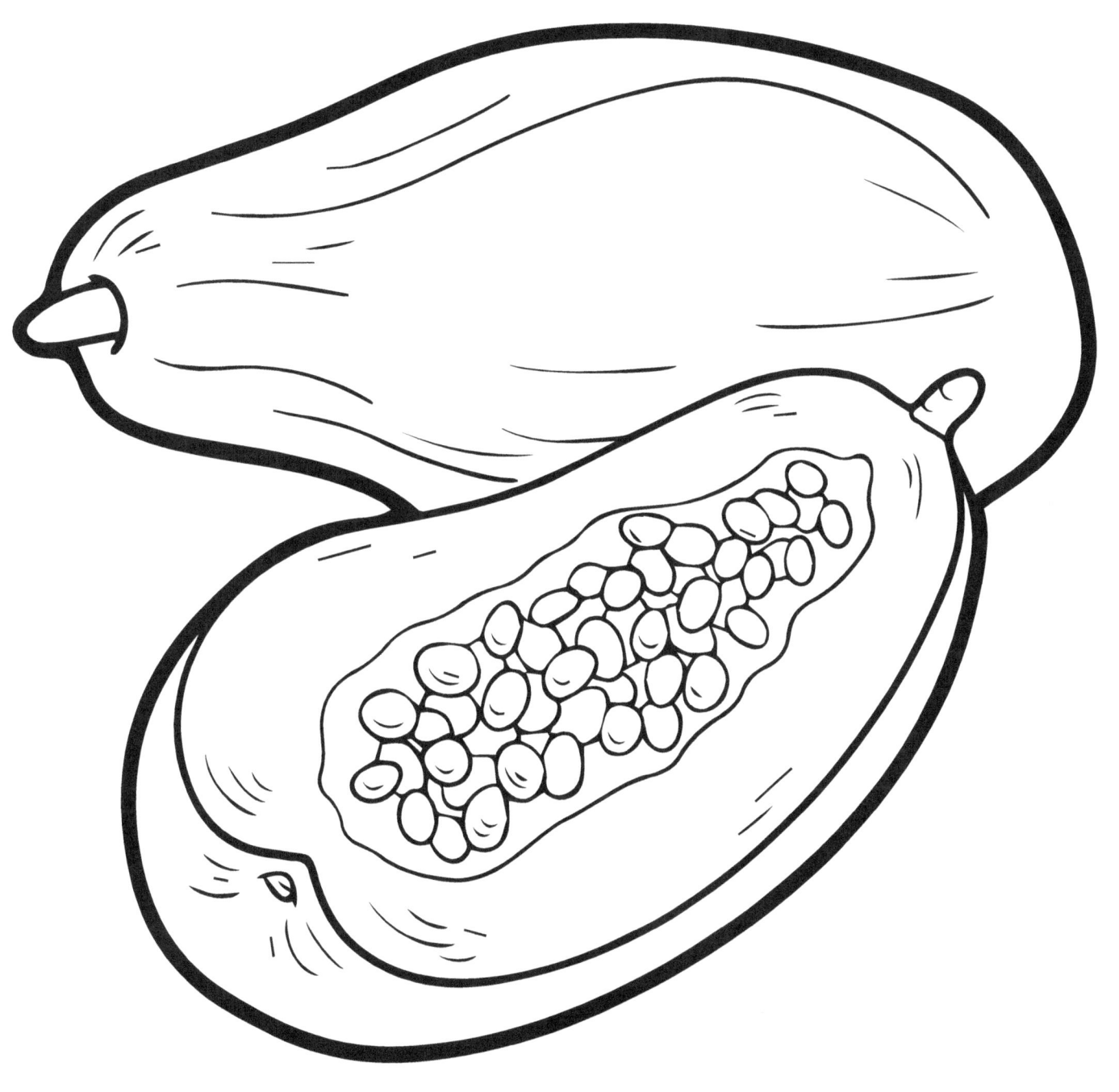

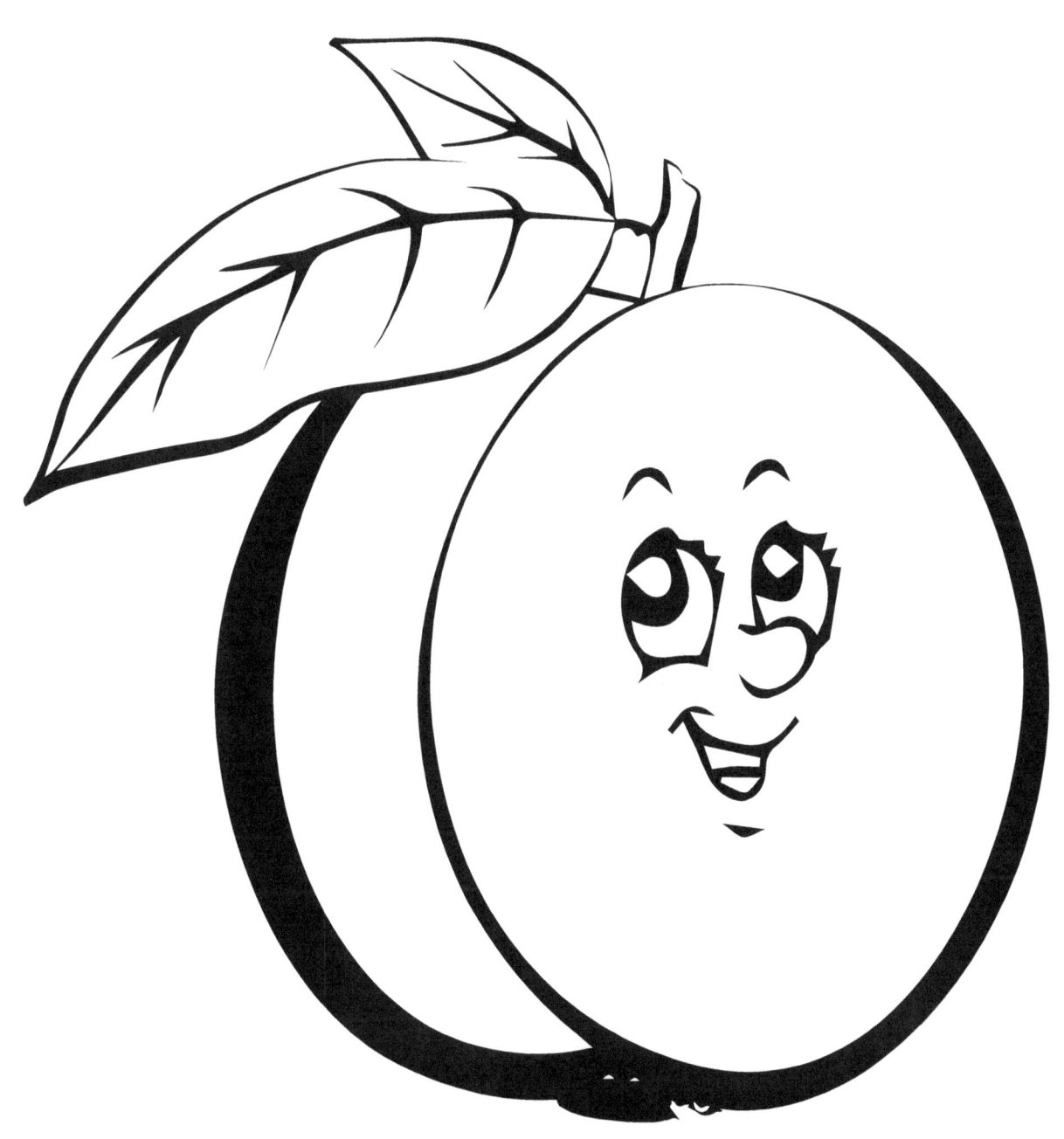

POMEGRANATE

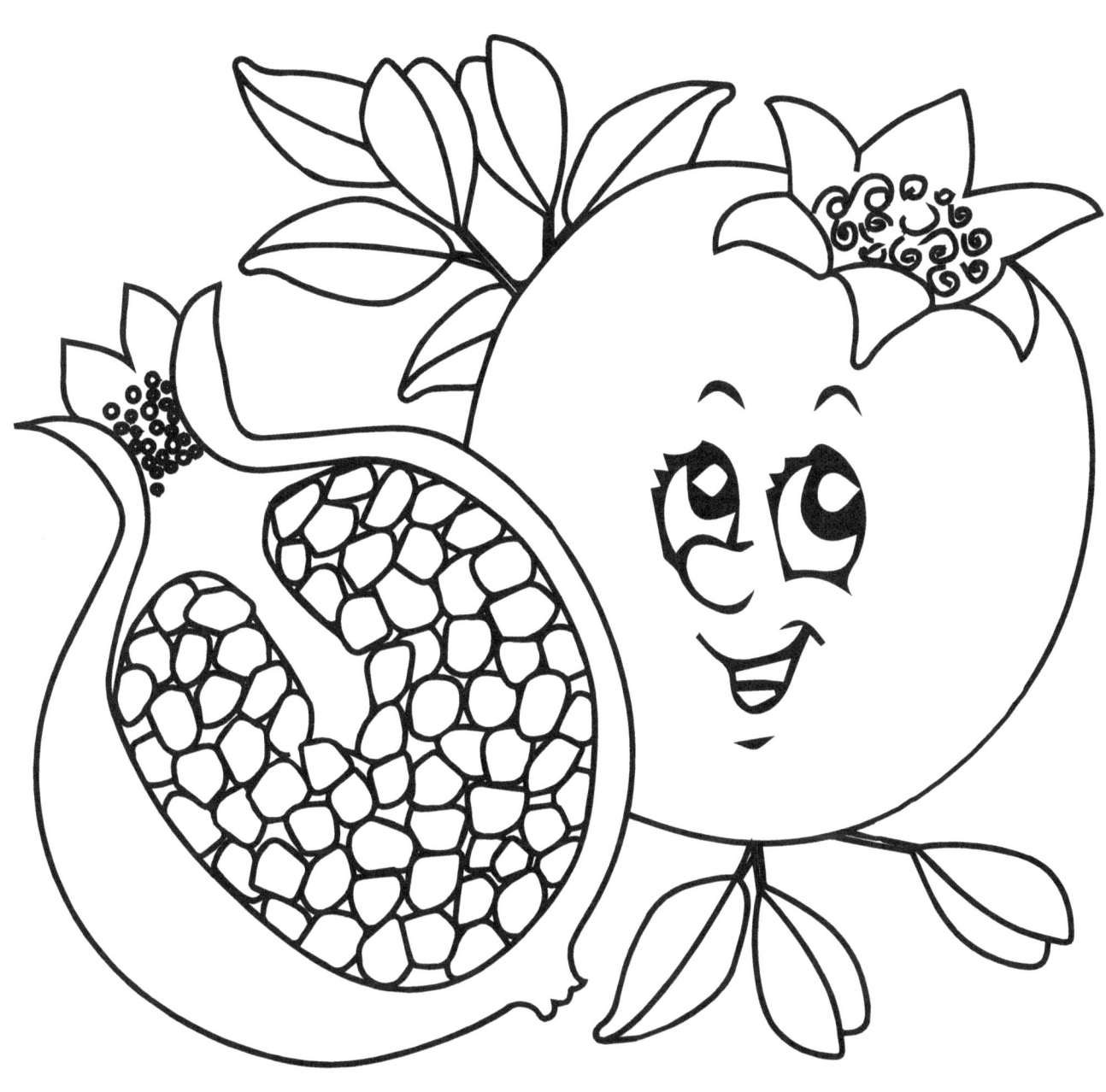

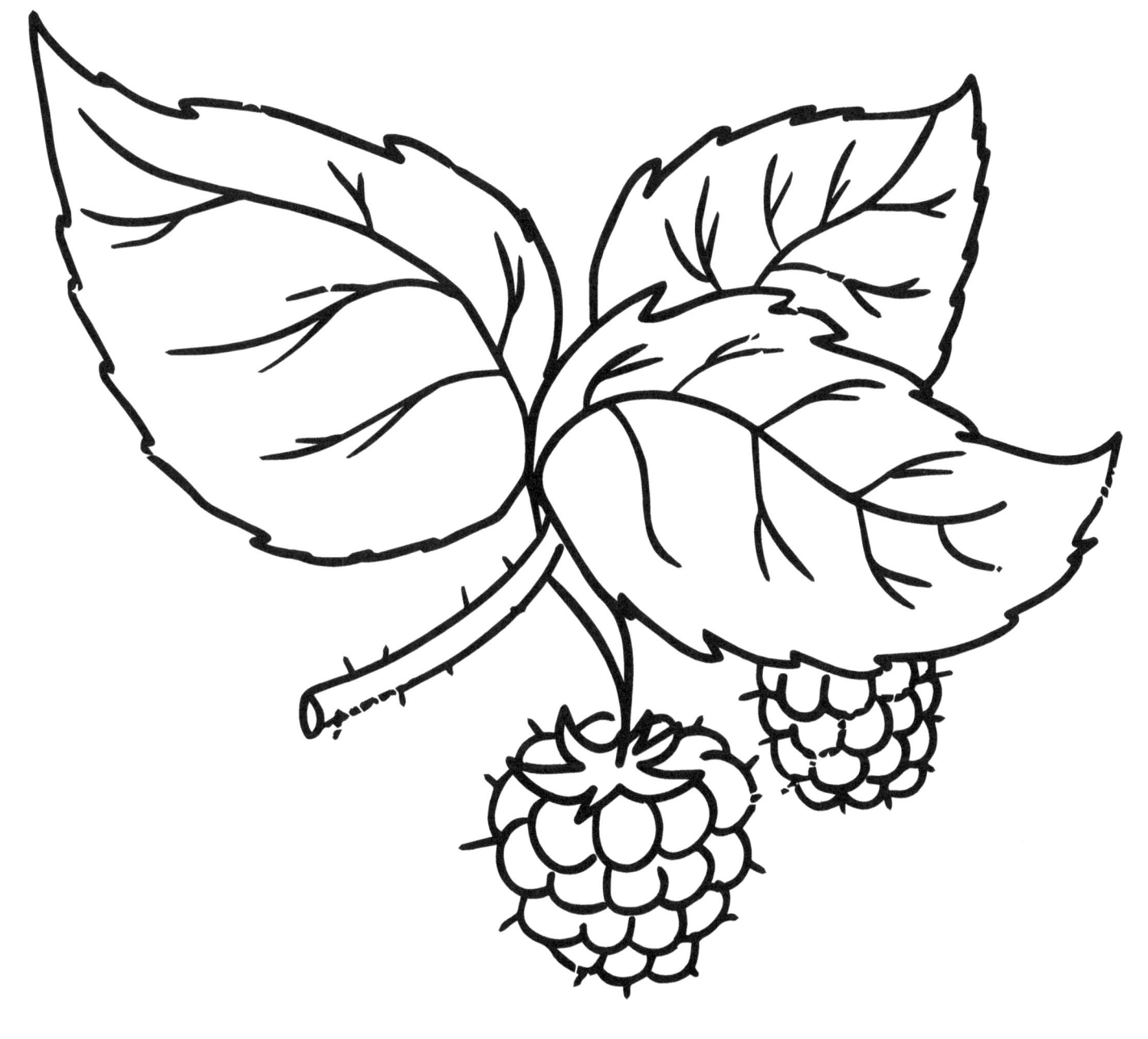

what is my name

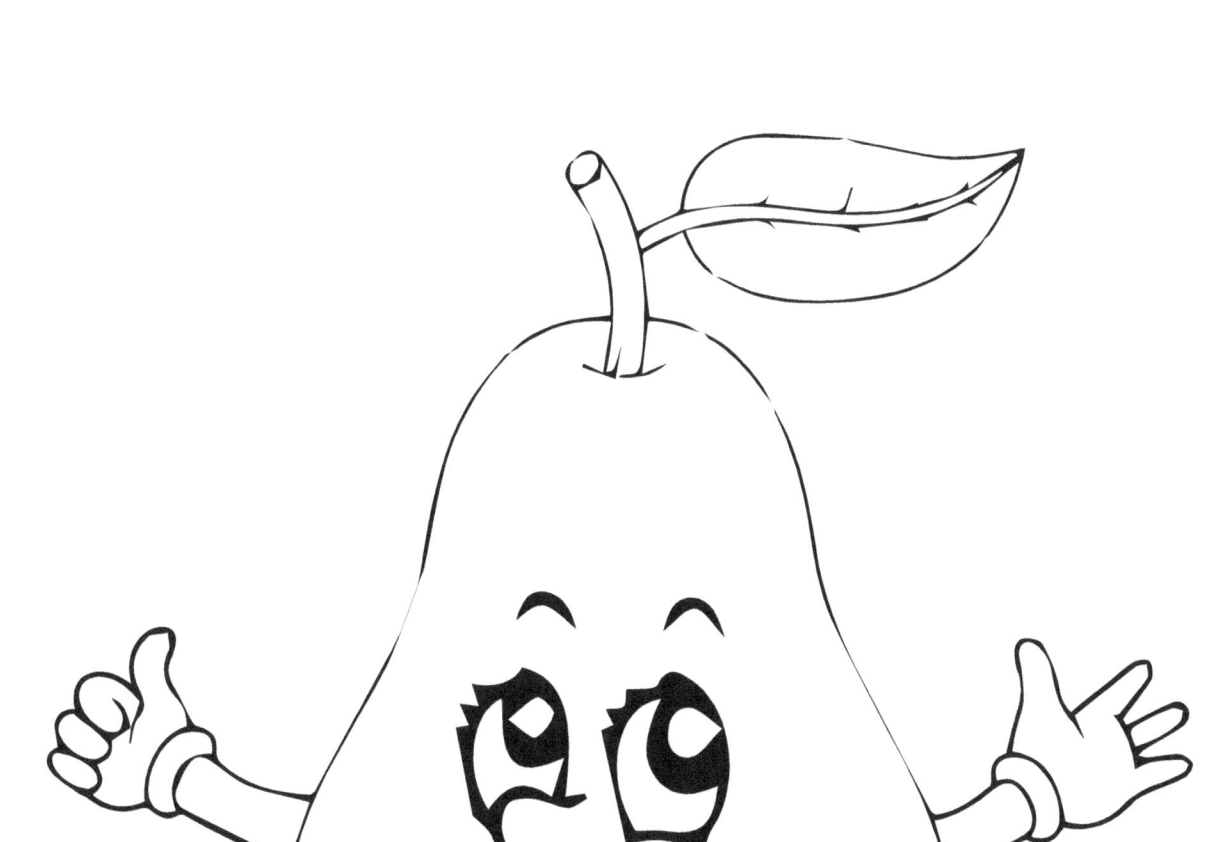

STRAWBE.........Y

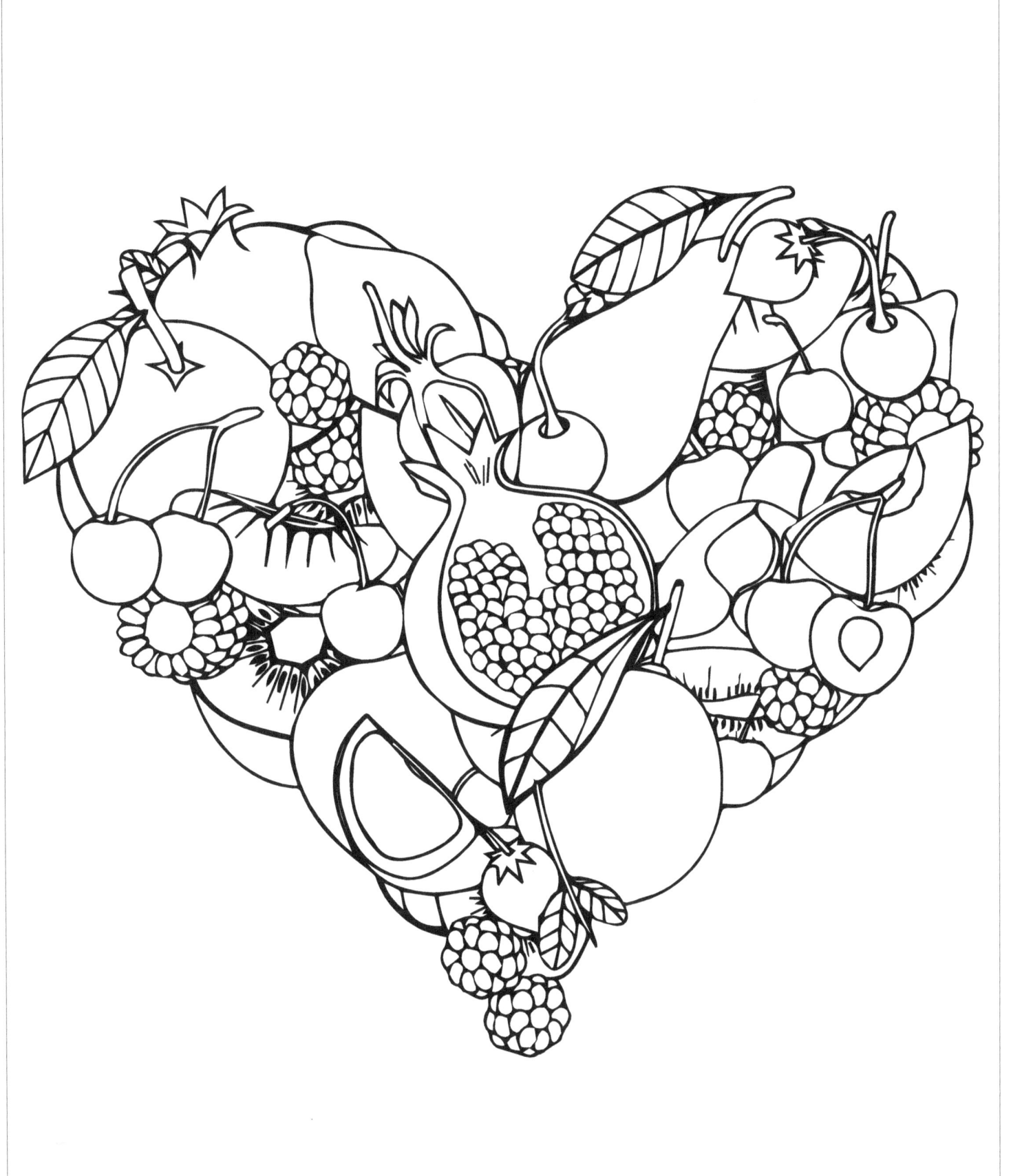

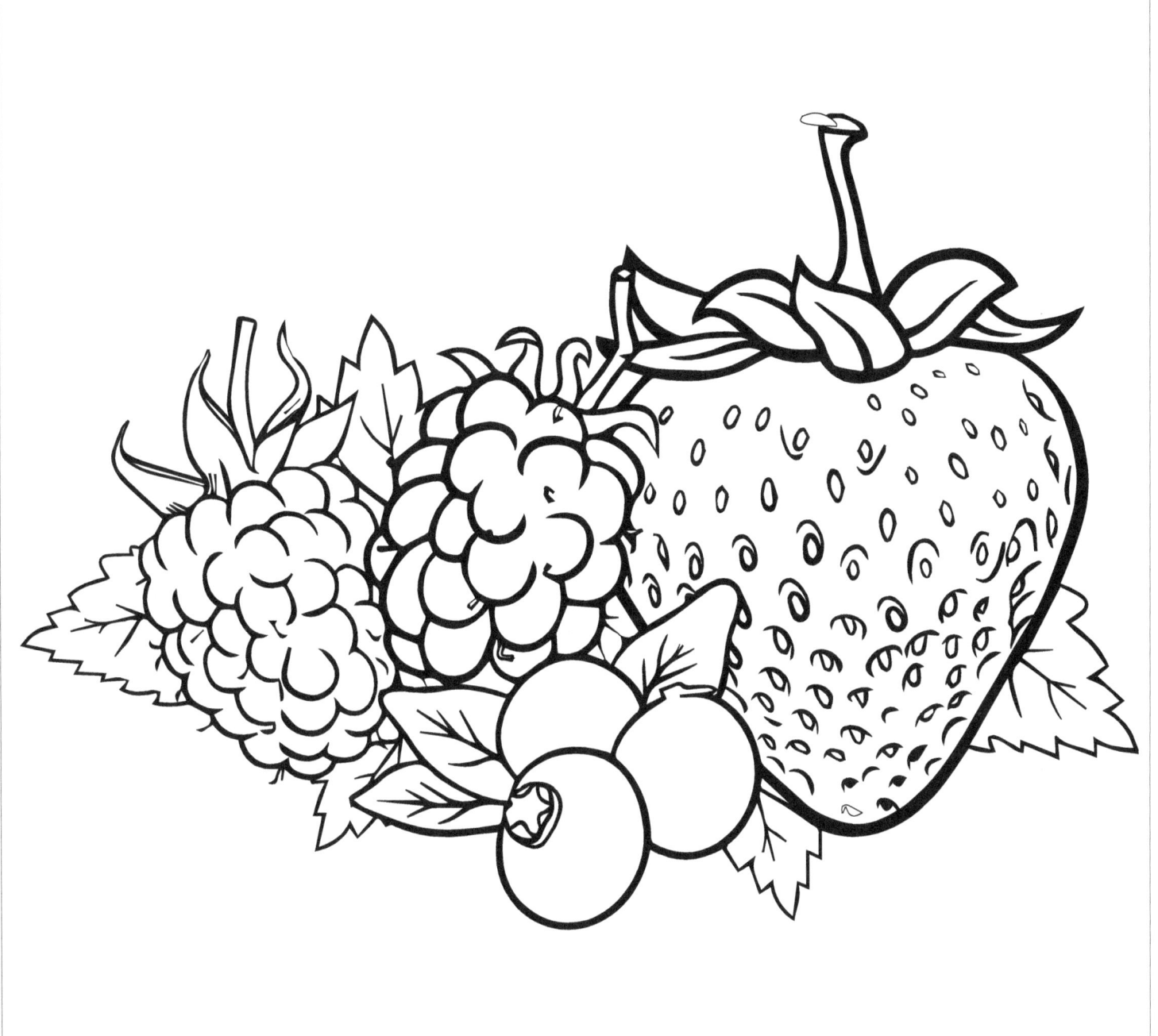

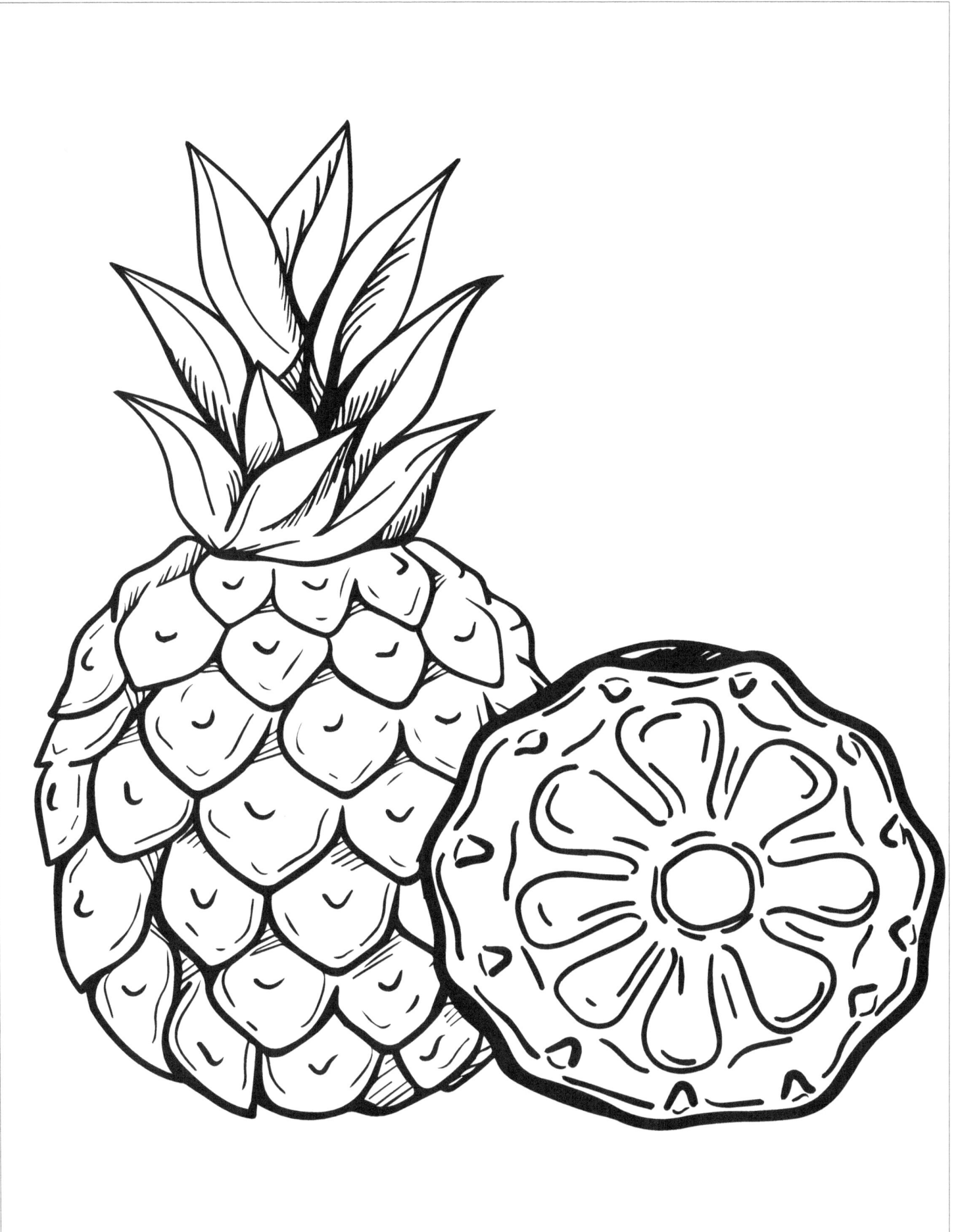

what is my name

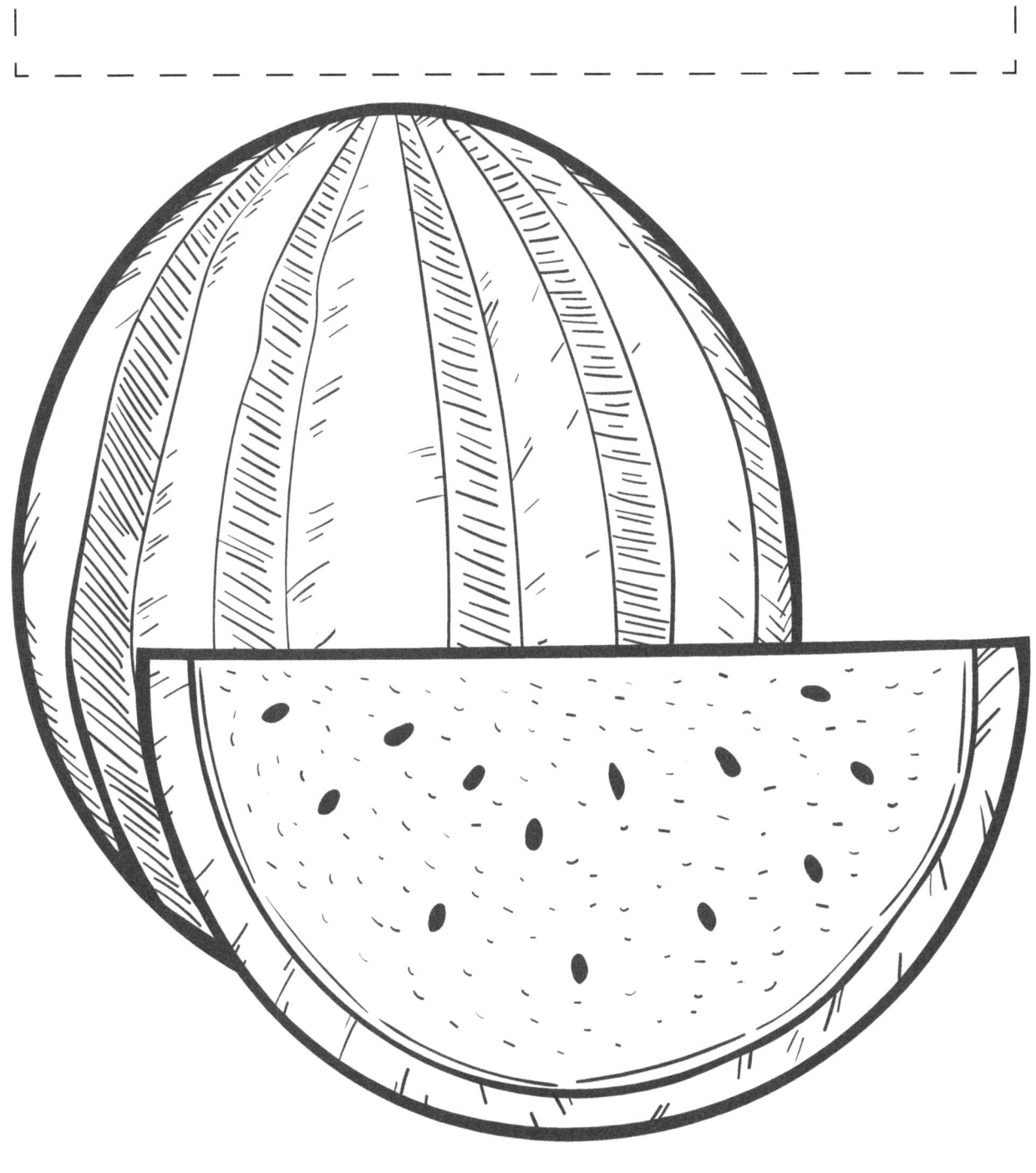

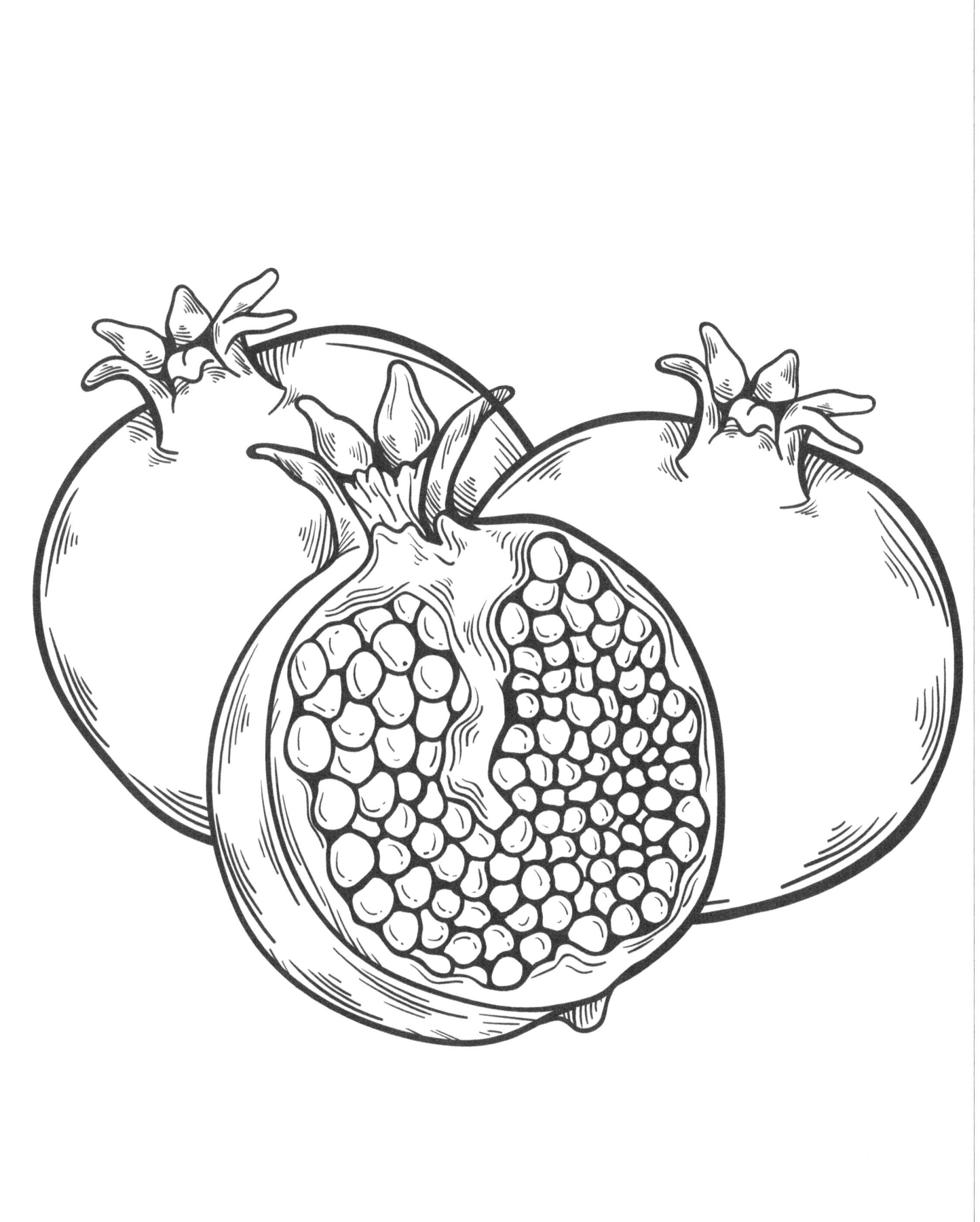

YOU ARE THE CHAMPION OF FRUITS

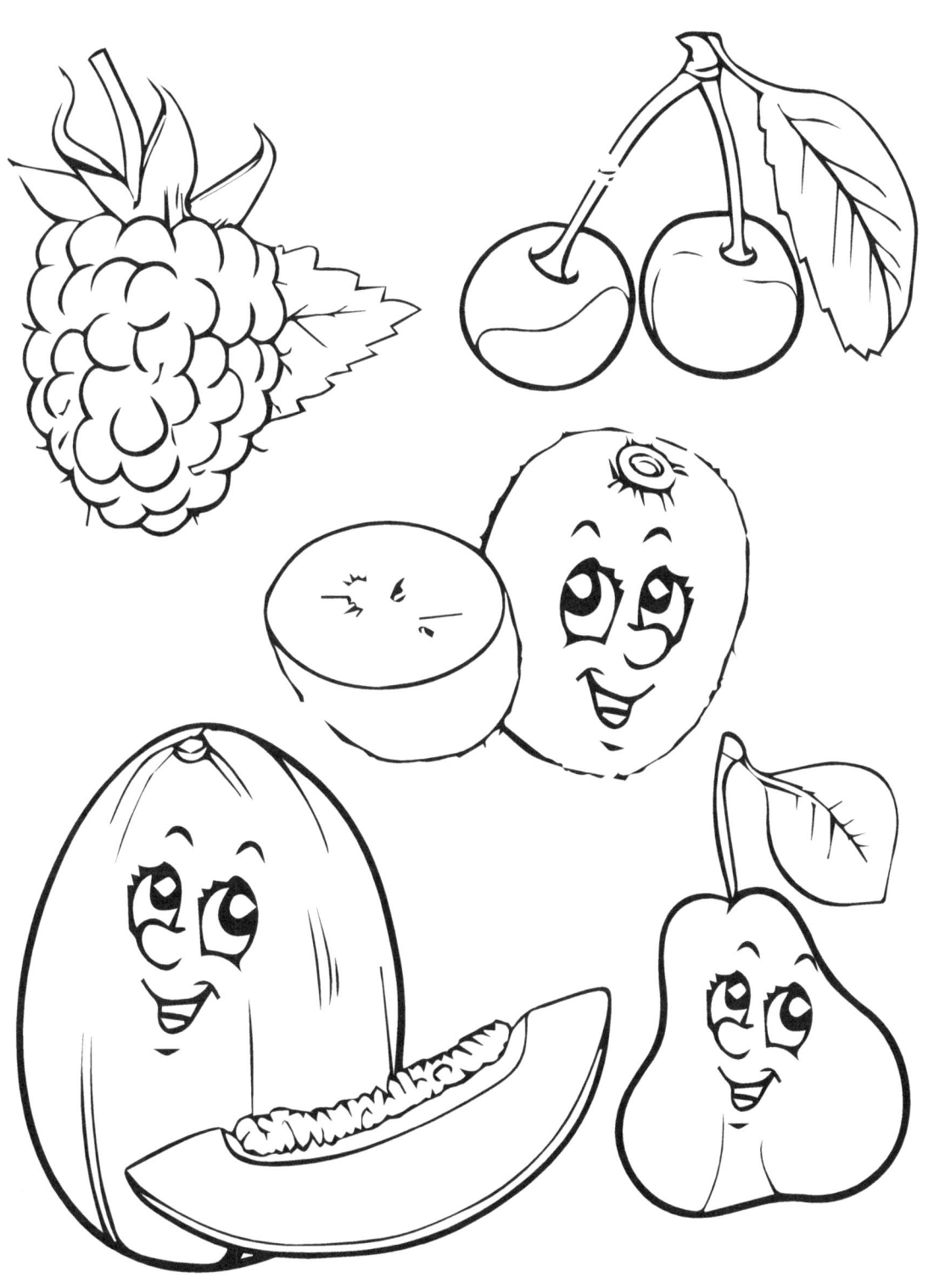

www.ingramcontent.com/pod-product-compliance
Lightning Source LLC
Chambersburg PA
CBHW080531220526
45465CB00006B/2665